D1681842

drawing for "DORKS"
"&" much more!

Cuter-than-Cute

Licensed exclusively to Imagine That Publishing Ltd
Tide Mill Way, Woodbridge, Suffolk, IP12 1AP, UK
www.imaginethat.com
Copyright © 2020 Imagine That Group Ltd
All rights reserved
0 2 4 6 8 9 7 5 3 1
Manufactured in Guangdong, China

IMAGINE THAT

DRAWING FOR DORKS QUIZ

How much of an artistic dork are you really? Take this fun quiz to find out and discover your inner dork!

1. My favorite kind of picture is...

   ☐ a. very colorful, with lots of things to look at.

   ☐ b. simple and calming—not many colors.

   ☐ c. a photo of a cute puppy or kitten!

2. If I were to draw a picture it would be...

   ☐ a. a herd of wild horses.

   ☐ b. a forest near the mountains.

   ☐ c. a cute pet or one of my friends!

3. My favorite color is...

   ☐ a. all of them!

   ☐ b. blues and greens.

   ☐ c. yellows and reds.

4. If I were to travel anywhere in the world to draw I would...

   ☐ a. visit a busy city, like New York or Tokyo.

   ☐ b. travel to the ocean or a tropical island.

   ☐ c. stay in a magical city, like Paris or Venice.

If you answered...

Mostly As

You are a super-adventurous artistic dork! There's no artistic challenge or color palette you are afraid of. Whether it's a city skyline or a wild animal, you'll draw anything you can see!

Mostly Bs

You are a super-chilled artistic dork! You take inspiration from nature to create calming works of art. Using a few colors at a time, you know less is often more. Your pictures even have a calming effect on anyone who sees them!

Mostly Cs

You are a super-imaginative artistic dork! You see the artistic potential in everyday things around you, but you aren't afraid to use your imagination and dream of far-away places!

Drawing Smarts

Follow these useful drawing tips as you create your cuter-than-cute works of art!

- Get comfortable! You can draw at a table, in the park, or you can even draw standing up waiting for a bus — just make sure you are comfortable before you start!

- Use a pencil to start your drawings. If you make a mistake, then you can easily erase it and start again.

- Don't worry if you do make a mistake — just remember to have fun!

- Drawing is mostly observation, so take time to study what you are drawing.

- Practice makes perfect!

Learn cute facts and create cuter-than-cute pictures in this how-to-draw section!

Puppy Love

Dork facts to amaze your BFs...

♥ Newborn puppies can't poop and need their mom to help them!

♥ Zzz. Zzz. Puppies nap for up to 15 hours a day.

♥ Puppies are born deaf and blind at birth.

♥ Just like human babies, puppies are born toothless!

♥ Some puppies in a light-colored litter can be born green!

♥ Dalmatian puppies are born without spots on their fur.

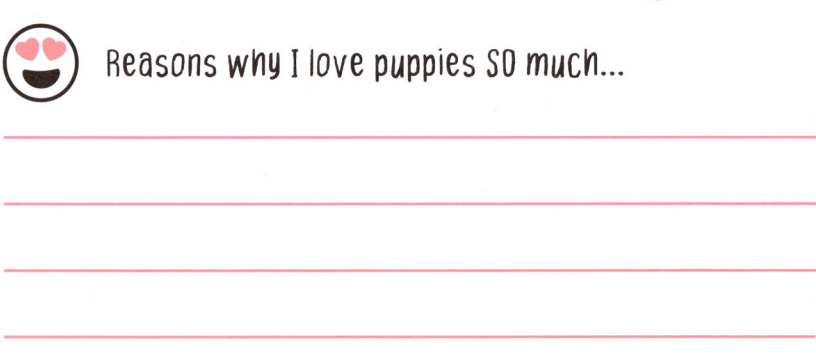

Reasons why I love puppies SO much...

_____
_____
_____
_____
_____

1

2

3

4

5

6

YOUR TURN!

Little Elephant

Dork facts to amaze your BFs...

♥ A baby elephant is called a calf.

♥ Elephants are the world's largest land animal!

♥ An elephant's trunk is actually both its nose and its upper lip!

♥ Elephants spend 12 to 18 hours every day eating grass, fruit, and plants.

♥ Nearly all baby elephants are born at night!

♥ Elephant tusks never stop growing. So, the longer the tusk—the older the elephant!

😍 Reasons why I love elephants SO much...

_____
_____
_____
_____
_____

1
2
3
4
5
6

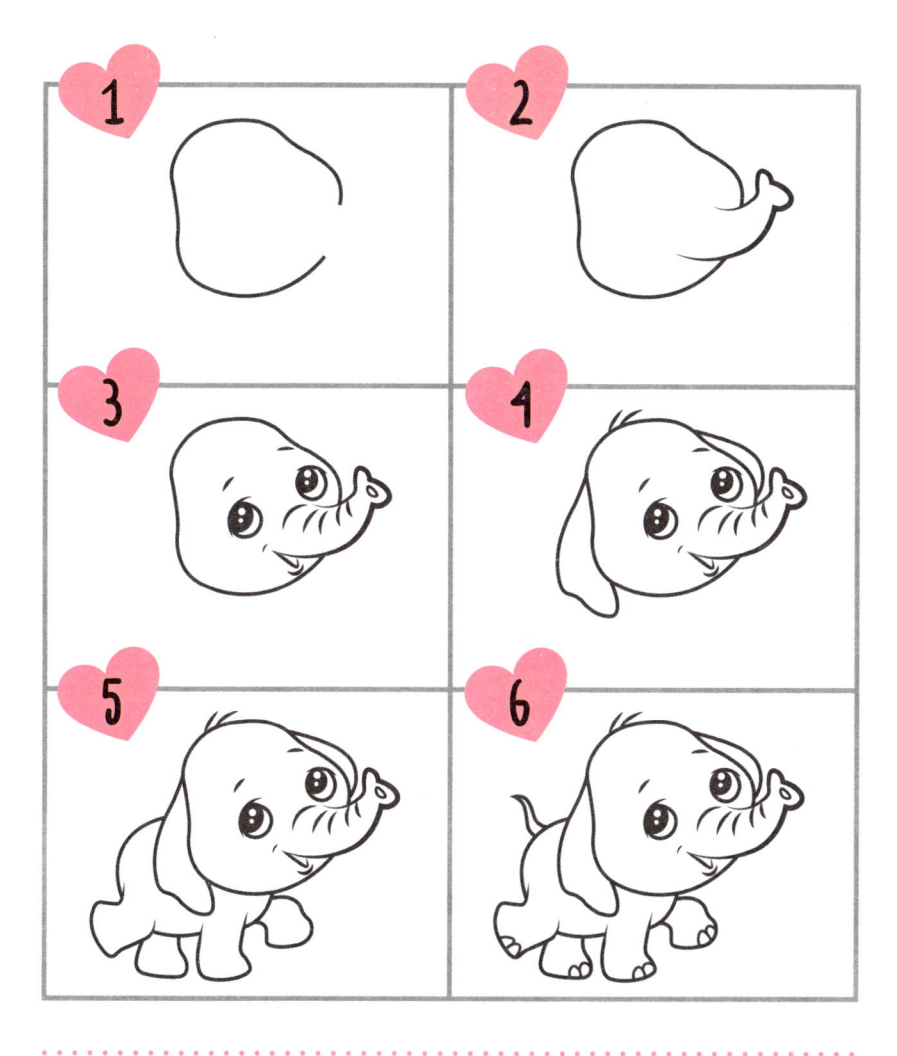

YOUR TURN!

Cupcake Cutie

Dork facts to amaze your BFs...

💗 Cupcakes are very popular. Over 700 million cupcakes are eaten in the US every year!

💗 The world's largest cupcake weighed over 2,500 pounds and was over 4 feet wide!

💗 In the 1700s, people baked little cakes in small cups—they became known as cupcakes!

💗 Cupcakes are also known as fairy cakes, patty cakes, and butterfly cakes.

💗 There's a special ATM in Los Angeles where you can buy cupcakes 24 hours a day!

💗 Cupcakes can be sweet with vanilla, chocolate, and fruit fillings, or they can be savory, flavored with cheese, chili pepper, anything you wish!

Reasons why I love cupcakes so much...

_____

_____

_____

1

2

3

4

5

6

YOUR TURN!

Flutterby Butterfly

Dork facts to amaze your BFs...

💗 There are between 15,000 and 20,000 different species of butterfly.

💗 Butterflies have taste receptors—tongues—on their feet!

💗 Butterflies can be found all over the world, except in Antarctica.

💗 Butterflies come in many sizes; the smallest is 1 inch long and the longest is 11 inches long!

💗 Skipper butterflies are fast fliers, flying at 37 miles per hour.

💗 Butterflies are unable to fly at temperatures below 55°F.

Reasons why I love butterflies so much...

_____
_____
_____
_____
_____

1

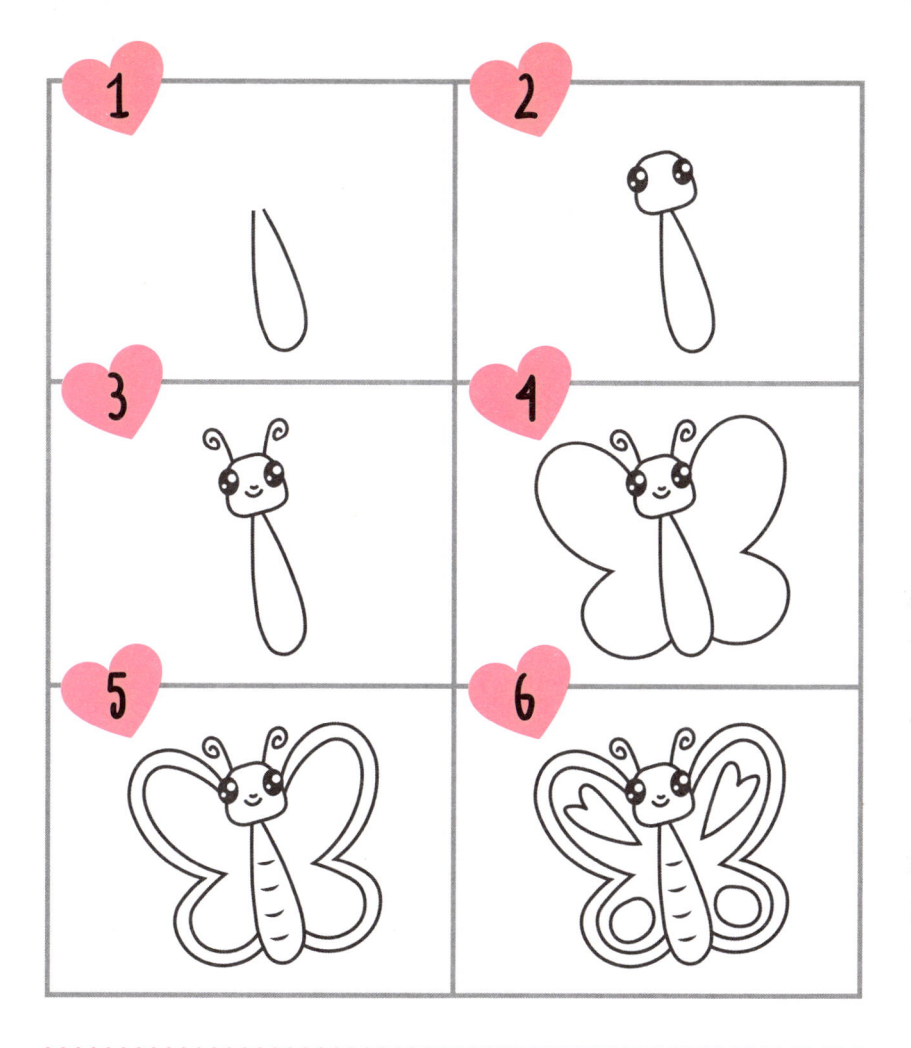

2

3

4

5

6

YOUR TURN!

SWISHY FISHY

Dork facts to amaze your BFs...

💗 Fish are found wherever there is water—from high mountain streams to deep oceans.

💗 There are over 30,000 known species of fish!

💗 The largest fish in the world is the whale shark. It's as long as a lorry!

💗 Most fish reproduce by laying eggs, though some fish, such as some species of sharks, give birth to live babies.

💗 A group of fish who swim together are called a school. Schools can contain over a million fish!

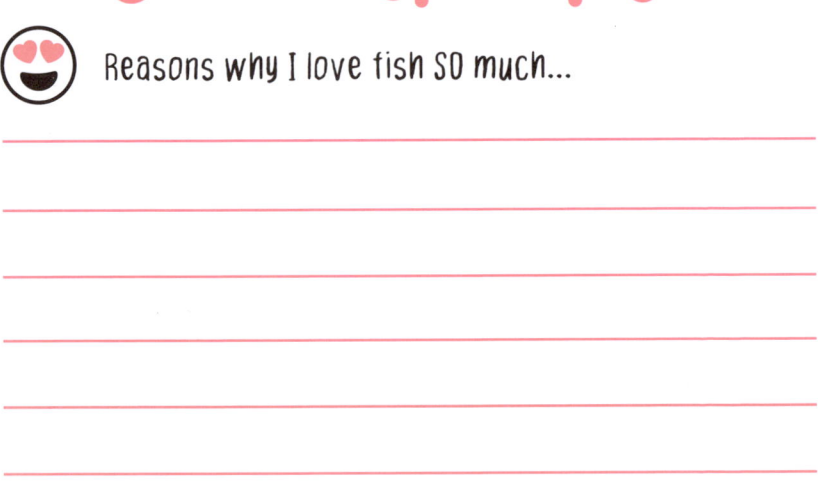

😍 Reasons why I love fish SO much...

_____
_____
_____
_____
_____
_____
_____

1 **2** **3** **4** **5** **6**

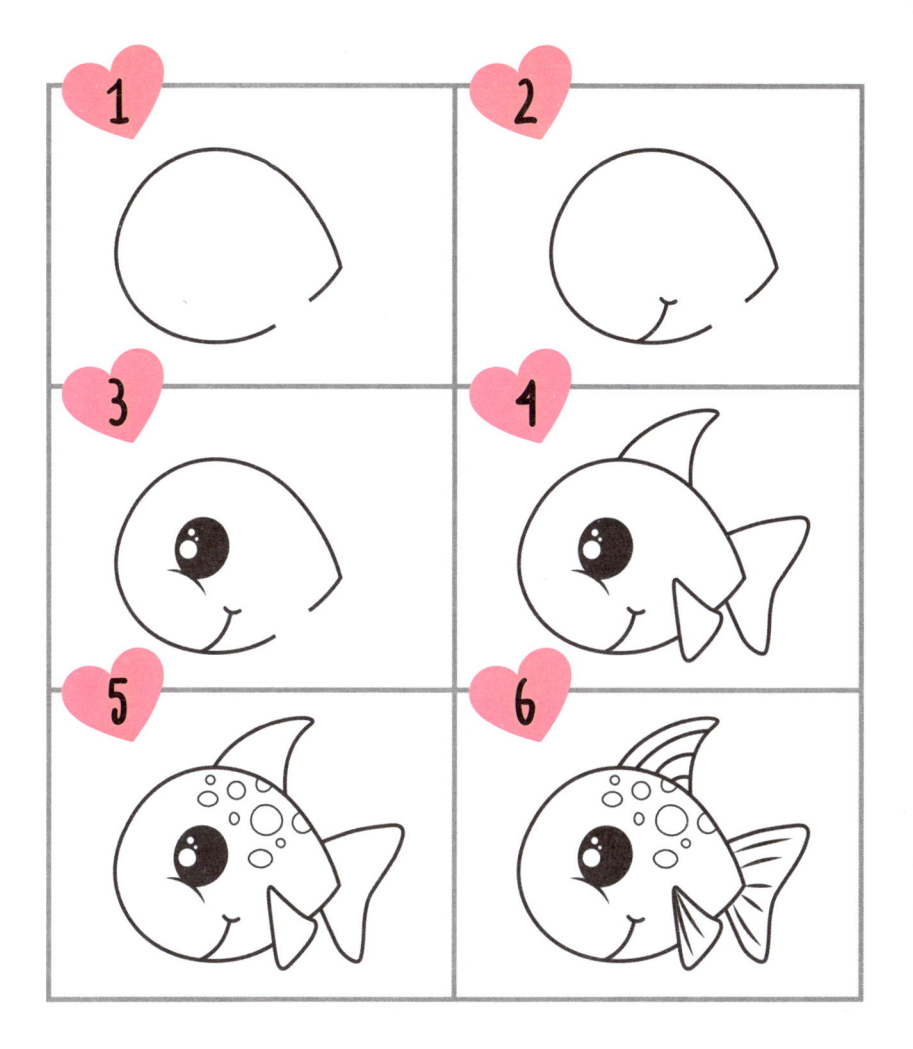

YOUR TURN!

Princess Cutie Pie

Dork facts to amaze your BFs...

- 💗 A princess is a member of a royal family.

- 💗 The son of a king or queen is called a prince.

- 💗 Princesses wear crowns or tiaras when attending formal occasions like concerts or balls.

- 💗 Princesses have many jobs. Many help charities or work to help others.

- 💗 There are princesses in most countries around the world.

- 💗 Cinderella is the most famous make-believe princess in the world.

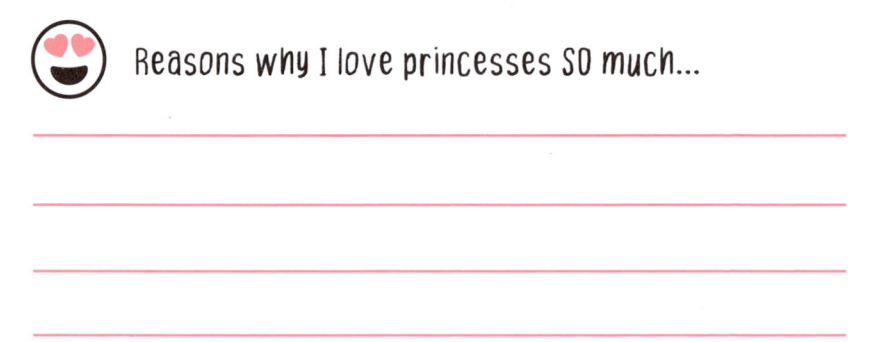

Reasons why I love princesses SO much...

_____
_____
_____
_____
_____

1
2
3
4
5
6

YOUR TURN!

flick the fairy

Dork facts to amaze your BFs...

♥ Fairies are small, magical creatures, who are believed to live in the forests.

♥ Fairies are said to use their magic to protect all the creatures who live among the flowers and the trees.

♥ Fairies have bright, colorful wings like a butterfly.

♥ Fairies like to remain hidden from human sight, but sometimes you can hear them as they flutter past.

♥ The Queen of the fairies has a magical wand, which is powerful enough to make any wish come true.

♥ The tooth fairy is the most famous fairy of all.

Reasons why I love fairies SO much...

_____
_____
_____
_____
_____

1
2
3
4
5
6

YOUR TURN!

Pretty Kitty

Dork facts to amaze your BFs...

♥ Cats can sleep for about 12 to 14 hours a day.

♥ Ancient Egyptians may have been the first to have pet cats nearly 4,000 years ago.

♥ There are many cat breeds such as the Maine Coon, Japanese Bobtail, Norwegian Forest Cat, and the Australian Mist.

♥ The Manx cat is best known for having a small stubby tail, instead of a long one.

♥ A cat's eyes reflect light, allowing them to see prey easily at night.

♥ A cat's long tail helps it to balance, especially when running fast or leaping from one place to another.

Reasons why I love cats so much...

_____
_____
_____
_____

1

2

3

4

5

6

YOUR TURN!

Little Frog

Dork facts to amaze your BFS...

💗 Frogs are amphibians; they need to live in or near water to survive.

💗 Frogs can breathe and absorb water through their skin.

💗 Some species of frog in Central and South America, like the poison dart frog have brightly-colored, toxic skin and are highly poisonous.

💗 Frogs lay eggs, called frogspawn in water. When the eggs hatch, the larvae are called tadpoles.

💗 Tadpoles have tails to help them survive in water. As they become adult frogs they lose their tadpole tails.

💗 Flying frogs are also called parachute frogs. Their webbed feet help them to glide through the air when they leap from branch to branch.

Reasons why I love frogs so much...

_____
_____
_____

1
2
3
4
5
6

YOUR TURN!

Flying Unicorn

Dork facts to amaze your BFs...

♥ Unicorns look very similar to horses, except a unicorn has a magical horn on its forehead.

♥ There are many stories and legends about unicorns. People once thought rhinos were unicorns!

♥ Unicorns do not have wings. There is a famous legend about a winged horse called Pegasus.

♥ Many once thought that narwhals were unicorns of the sea, because of their long horns.

♥ A unicorn's favorite snack is a colorful rainbow oat cookie sprinkled with stardust.

Reasons why I love unicorns so much...

_____
_____
_____
_____
_____

1
2
3
4
5
6

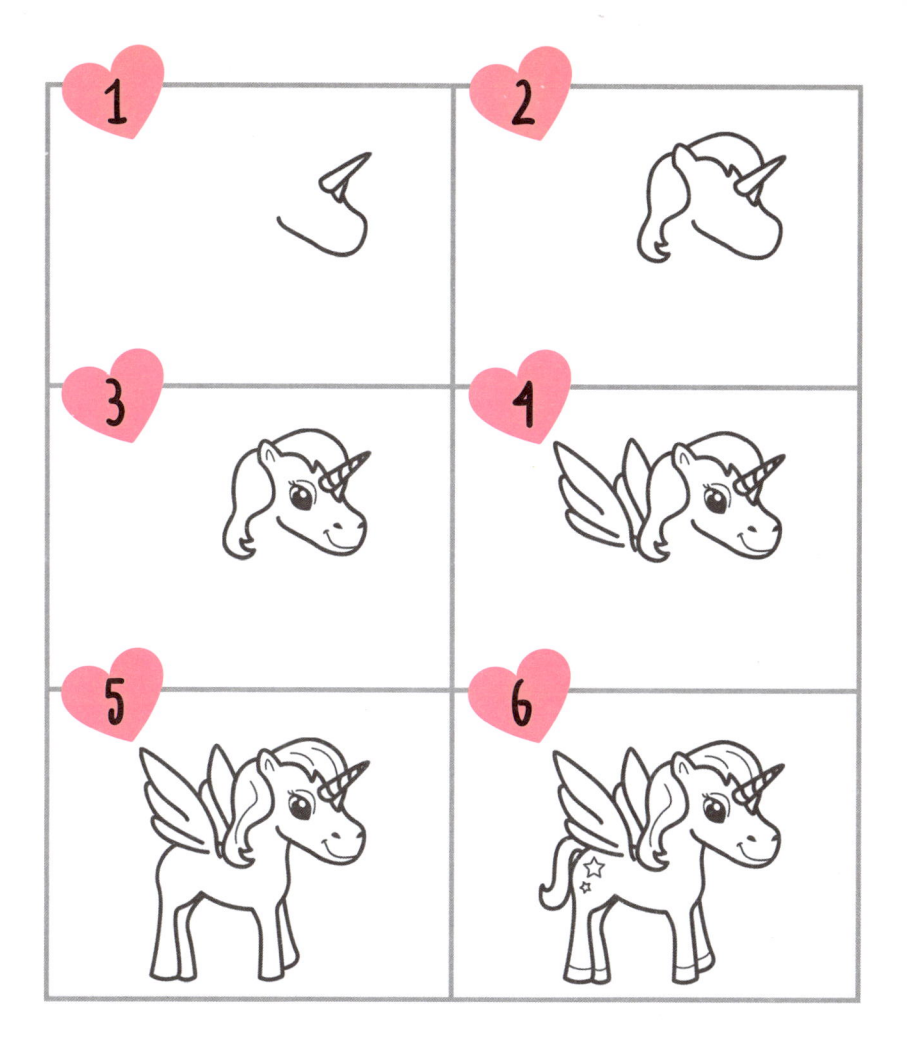

YOUR TURN!

Bear Cub

Dork facts to amaze your BFs...

💗 Bears are found throughout North and South America, Europe, and Asia.

💗 The smallest bear is the sun bear, it is 4 feet long and weighs nearly 60 pounds.

💗 The biggest bear is the polar bear, which grows to 8 feet long and over 1,000 pounds.

💗 The eight species of bear are Asiatic black bears, brown bears, giant pandas, North American black bears, polar bears, sloth bears, spectacled bears, and sun bears.

💗 During the winter hibernation months, grizzly bears and black bears can go without food and water for 100 days.

💗 Sadly, six of the eight species of bear are listed as vulnerable or threatened due to loss of habitat.

Reasons why I love bears so much...

_____
_____
_____

1	2
3	4
5	6

YOUR TURN!

Baby Penguin

Dork facts to amaze your BFs...

♥ All 18 different species of penguins have black bodies and wings and white bellies.

♥ The largest penguin is the emperor penguin. It grows to 4 feet tall. The smallest is the fairy penguin at 1 foot tall.

♥ Penguins are only found in the southern hemisphere, with most living in or near Antarctica.

♥ A penguin's flippers and streamline shape make them fast swimmers. They can swim about 15 miles in an hour.

♥ Penguins spend nearly all their lives in the ocean, where they hunt for prey like squid, crabs, and krill.

♥ On land penguins huddle together in large colonies. Here they lay eggs and raise their young.

Reasons why I love penguins SO much...

_____
_____
_____

1 2 3 4 5 6

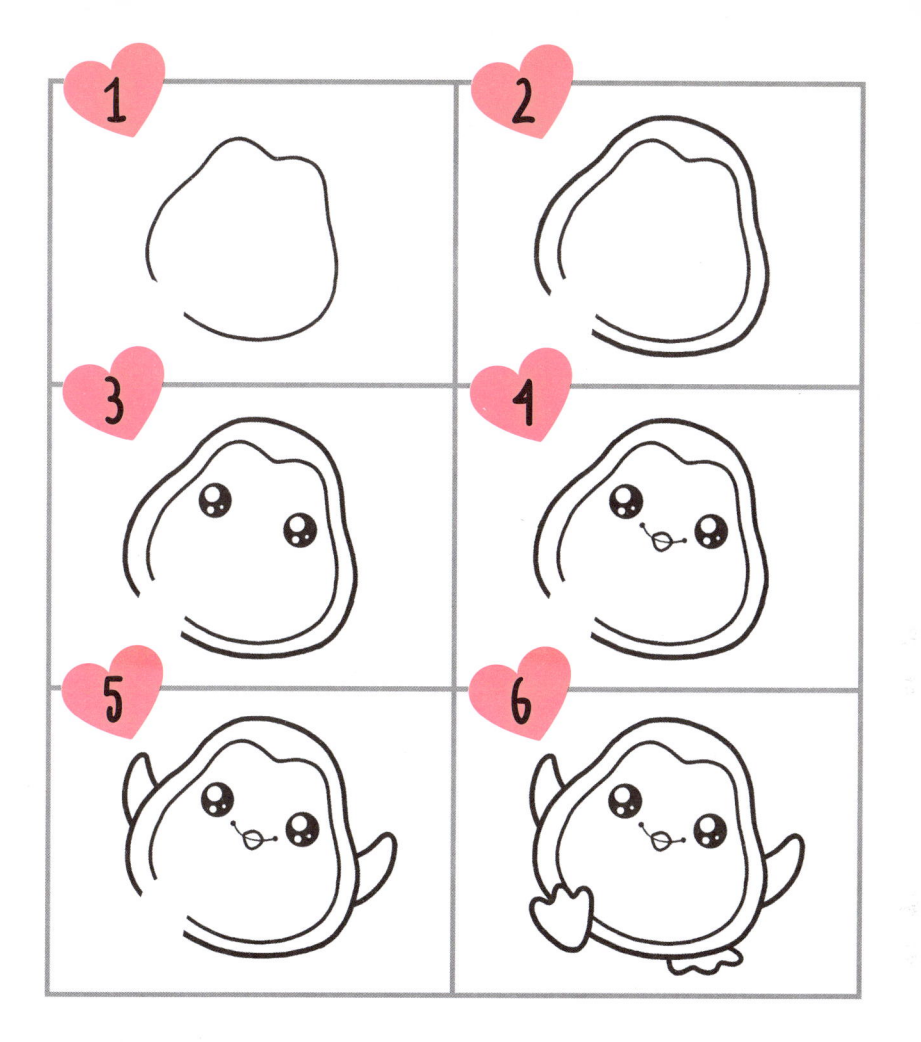

YOUR TURN!

Wobble the Octopus

Dork facts to amaze your BFs...

💗 Octopuses are found all over the world's oceans, but they mostly live in warm waters.

💗 An octopus has eight arms, each lined with suckers that they use to pull prey into their mouth.

💗 Octopuses can swim backward by blasting water through a muscular tube on their body called a siphon!

💗 When an octopus is threatened, they shoot inky fluid from their body to darken the water and make their escape.

💗 An octopus can change its skin color and texture to blend in with its surroundings.

💗 Octopuses live alone in dens that they build from rocks on the sea floor.

Reasons why I love octopuses so much...

_____
_____
_____
_____

1 **2**

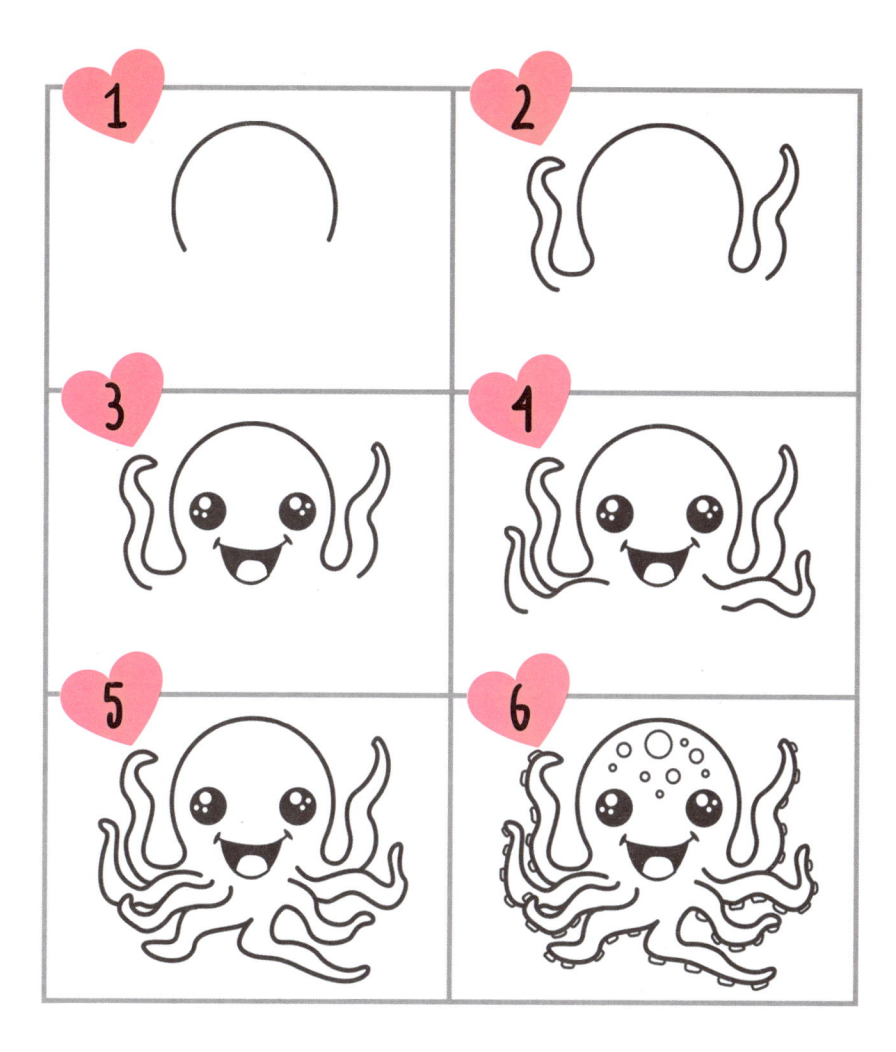

3 **4**

5 **6**

YOUR TURN!

Cute Koala

Dork facts to amaze your BFs...

- Koalas aren't bears, they are marsupials, like kangaroos and opossums.

- Koalas can be found wherever eucalyptus trees grow.

- When born, a baby koala is carried in its mother's pouch for six months.

- Koalas sleep in the trees during the day—some sleep for up to 18 hours!

- At night, koalas wake to feed on eucalyptus leaves, eating up to two and a half pounds of leaves in a single night!

- Koalas have pouches in their cheeks where they store food for snacks.

Reasons why I love koalas so much...

_____
_____
_____
_____

1
2
3
4
5
6

YOUR TURN!

Adorable Guinea Pig

Dork facts to amaze your BFs...

♥ Guinea pigs aren't pigs and they don't come from Guinea. They originally come from the Andes, South America.

♥ There are three types of guinea pigs—American, Abyssinian, and Peruvian!

♥ Guinea pigs love making noises to communicate! They squeak, chirp, grumble, and purr.

♥ A guinea pig's teeth grow continuously, so they have to chew and gnaw at food to prevent them from growing too long!

♥ Baby guinea pigs are called "pups."

Reasons why I love guinea pigs so much...

_____
_____
_____
_____

1

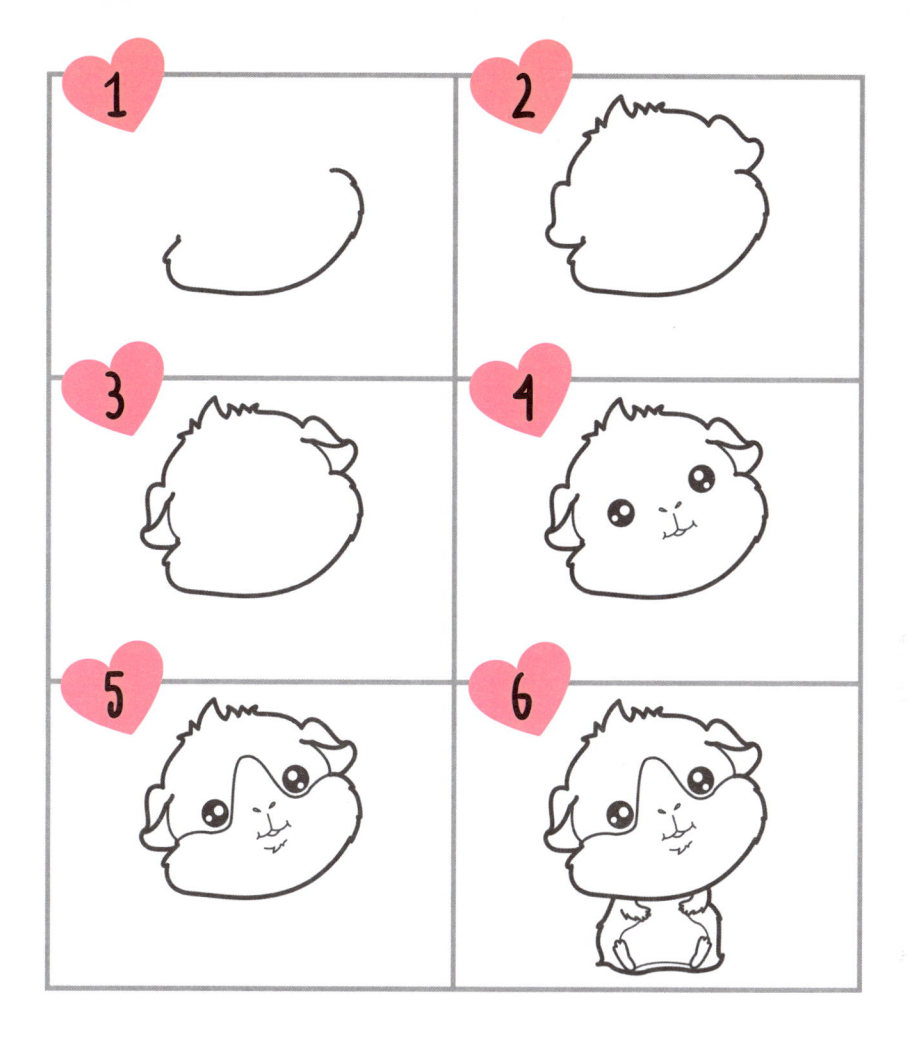

2

3

4

5

6

YOUR TURN!

Wonderful Waffles

Dork facts to amaze your BFs...

💗 The first waffles were eaten as long as 700 years ago. These thin pancakes were only eaten on special occasions.

💗 In the United States, August 24 is known as National Waffle Day! International Waffle Day is on March 25.

💗 The word "waffle" is from the Dutch word for "wafer."

💗 The world's largest waffle was made in the Netherlands in 2013. It was 8 feet wide and weighed 110 pounds.

💗 The world record for waffle eating is held by Patrick Bertoletti. In October 2007 he ate 29 waffles in 10 minutes!

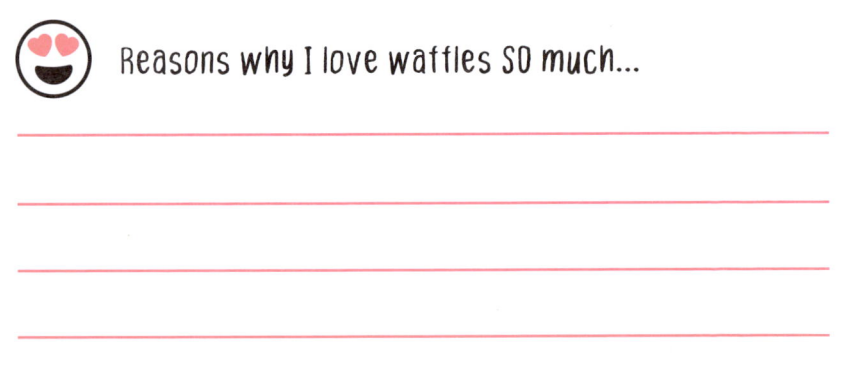

Reasons why I love waffles SO much...

_____
_____
_____
_____
_____

1
2
3
4
5
6

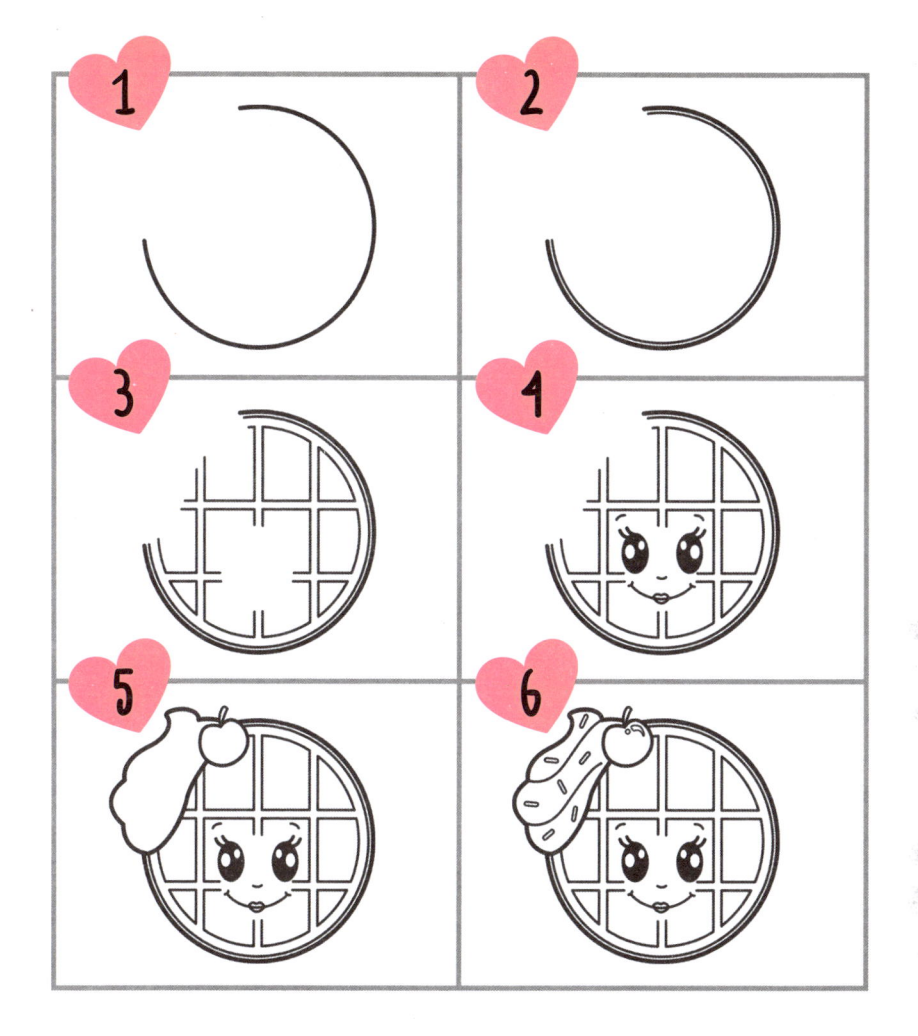

YOUR TURN!

Busy Bee

Dork facts to amaze your BFs...

♥ Honeybees have been used by humans for 9,000 years for their honey and beeswax.

♥ Honeybees live in a hive with one queen bee and hundreds of female worker bees and male drone bees.

♥ The queen bee lays eggs that become new bees to look after the hive.

♥ During spring and summer months, worker bees gather pollen and make honey to use for food in the winter.

♥ Beekeepers keep bees in wooden hives so they can collect and sell the honey the bees make.

😍 Reasons why I love bees so much...

_____
_____
_____
_____

1
2
3
4
5
6

YOUR TURN!

Polar Bear Cub

Dork facts to amaze your BFs...

- 💜 Polar bears are powerful predators, found in the coldest environments of the Northern hemisphere.

- 💜 Polar bears are the largest of all the bears. They are over 9 feet long and weigh up to 1,600 pounds.

- 💜 Polar bears are expert swimmers. Their large webbed front paws help them paddle underwater.

- 💜 Under their white fur, polar bears have black skin which soaks up warmth from the sun.

- 💜 The bottom of a polar bear's paws are covered in fur. This protects against the cold and helps them grip the ice.

Reasons why I love polar bears so much...

_____
_____
_____
_____

1 2
3 4
5 6

YOUR TURN!

Fiery Dragon

Dork facts to amaze your BFs...

- 💗 Dragons are mythical fire-breathing monsters, usually shown with large wings, scaly bodies, and a long tail.

- 💗 The word "dragon" comes from the Greek word "drakōn," which was used to describe a large serpent.

- 💗 Over a thousand years ago, Norse warriors from Scandinavia painted dragons on their shields and carved dragons' heads on their ships.

- 💗 In China and Japan, dragons are shown without wings, but they can still fly.

- 💗 Dragons are real! Venomous Komodo dragons weigh over 300 pounds, making them the heaviest lizards on Earth.

😍 Reasons why I love dragons so much...

_____
_____
_____
_____
_____

1

2

3

4

5

6

YOUR TURN!

Happy Hippo

Dork facts to amaze your BFs...

♥ The name "Hippopotamus" means "river horse."

♥ Hippos spend 16 hours a day in rivers or lakes to stay cool under the sun.

♥ At night, hippos travel on land to graze, sometimes walking 6 miles in one night.

♥ Hippos are good swimmers, able to hold their breath underwater for five minutes.

♥ When on land a hippo can run at speeds of 19 miles per hour, much faster than the average human.

😍 Reasons why I love hippos so much...

_____
_____
_____
_____
_____
_____

1 2 3 4 5 6

YOUR TURN!

Little Lion

Dork facts to amaze your BFs...

💗 Lions live in groups called prides. Each pride contains 10 to 15 lions.

💗 Lions are mostly found in sub-Saharan Africa but there is a species of forest lion found in northwest India.

💗 Female lions work together to hunt for food between dusk and dawn.

💗 While the females are hunting, a male lion will protect the pride and patrol its territory.

💗 An adult male lion's roar is so loud it can be heard up to 5 miles away!

💗 The long hair around a male lion's head is called a mane.

😍 Reasons why I love lions SO much...

_____
_____
_____
_____

1
2
3
4
5
6

YOUR TURN!

Use this page to draw some cute characters! What are their names?

Use pens or pencils to complete these cuter-than-cute pictures. There are some super-cute jokes too, to make you laugh out loud!

Why was Cinderella kicked off the team?

Because she kept running away from the ball!

What's my name?

....

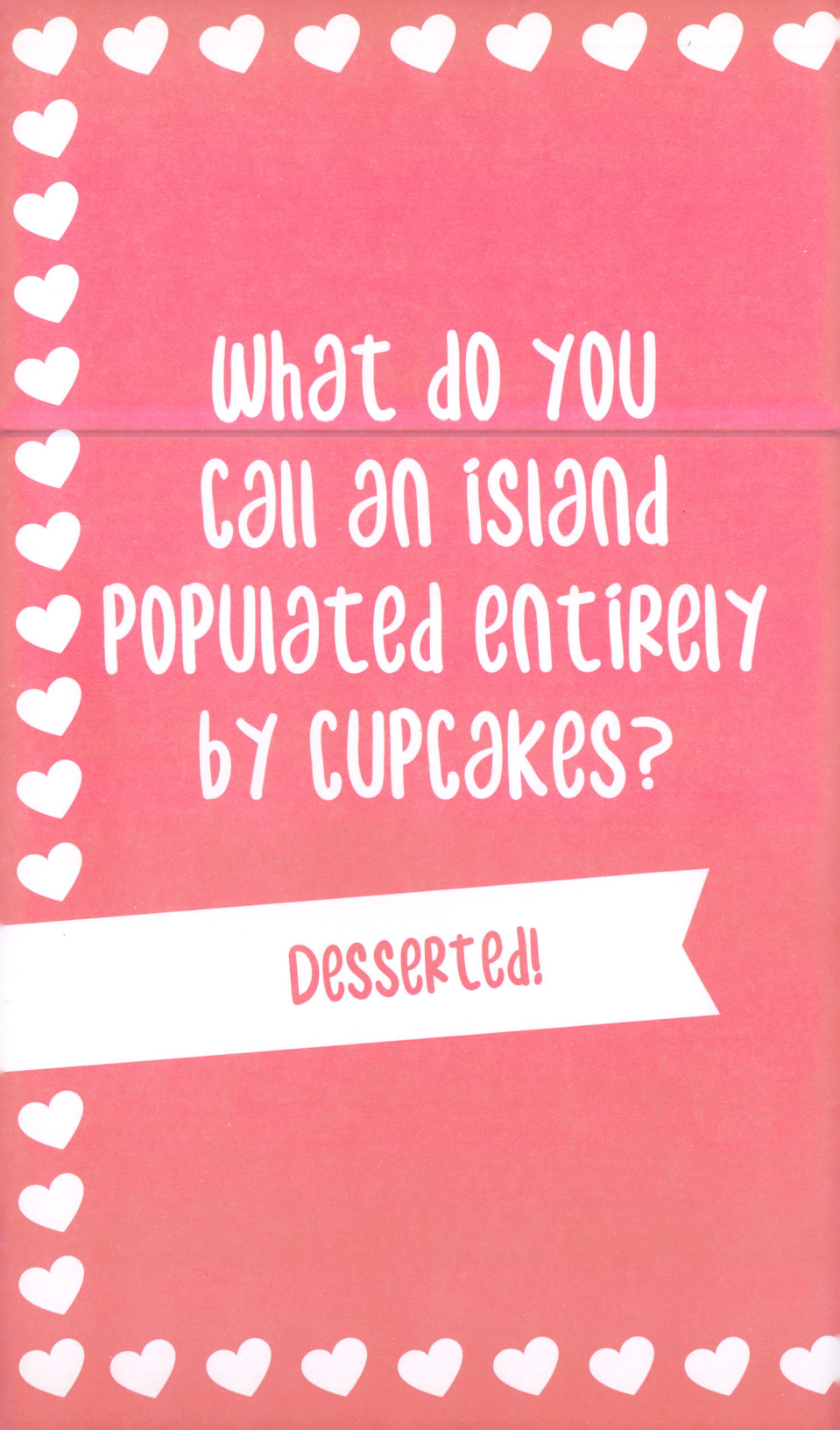

What do you call an island populated entirely by cupcakes?

Desserted!

What's my name?

....

What is blue and very big?

An elephant

holding its

breath!

What's my name?

....

What's the difference between a guitar and a fish?

You can't tuna fish!

What's my name?

....

What dog loves to take bubble baths?

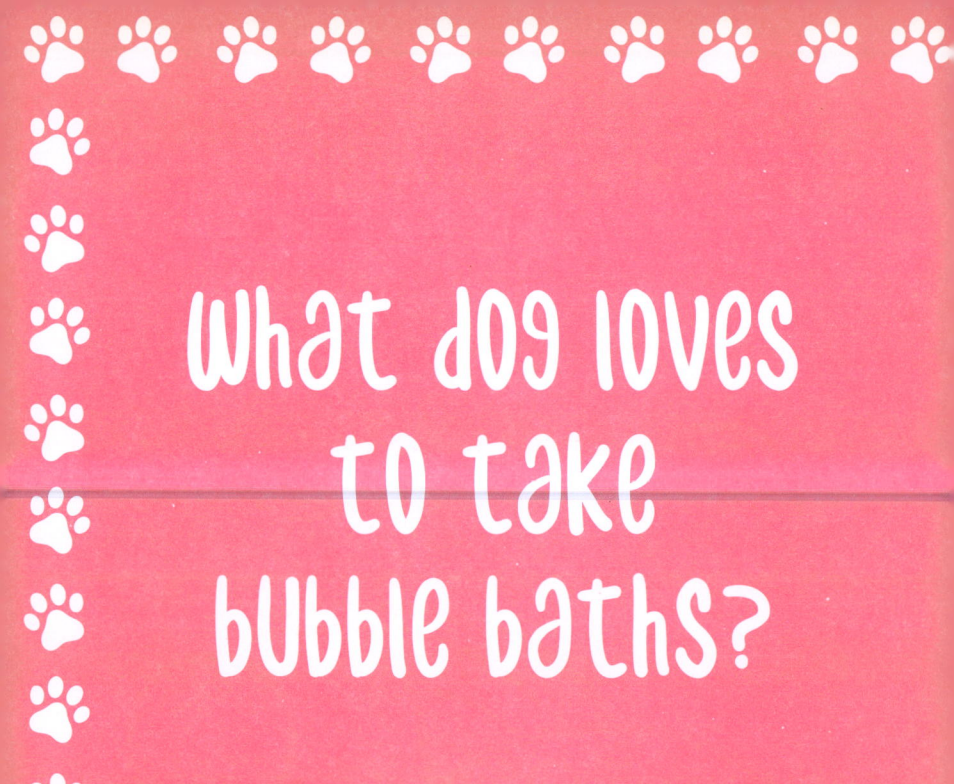

A shampoodle!

What's my name?

....

How do you make a butterfly?

> Throw the butter out the window!

what's my name?

....

Which day do lions eat the most?

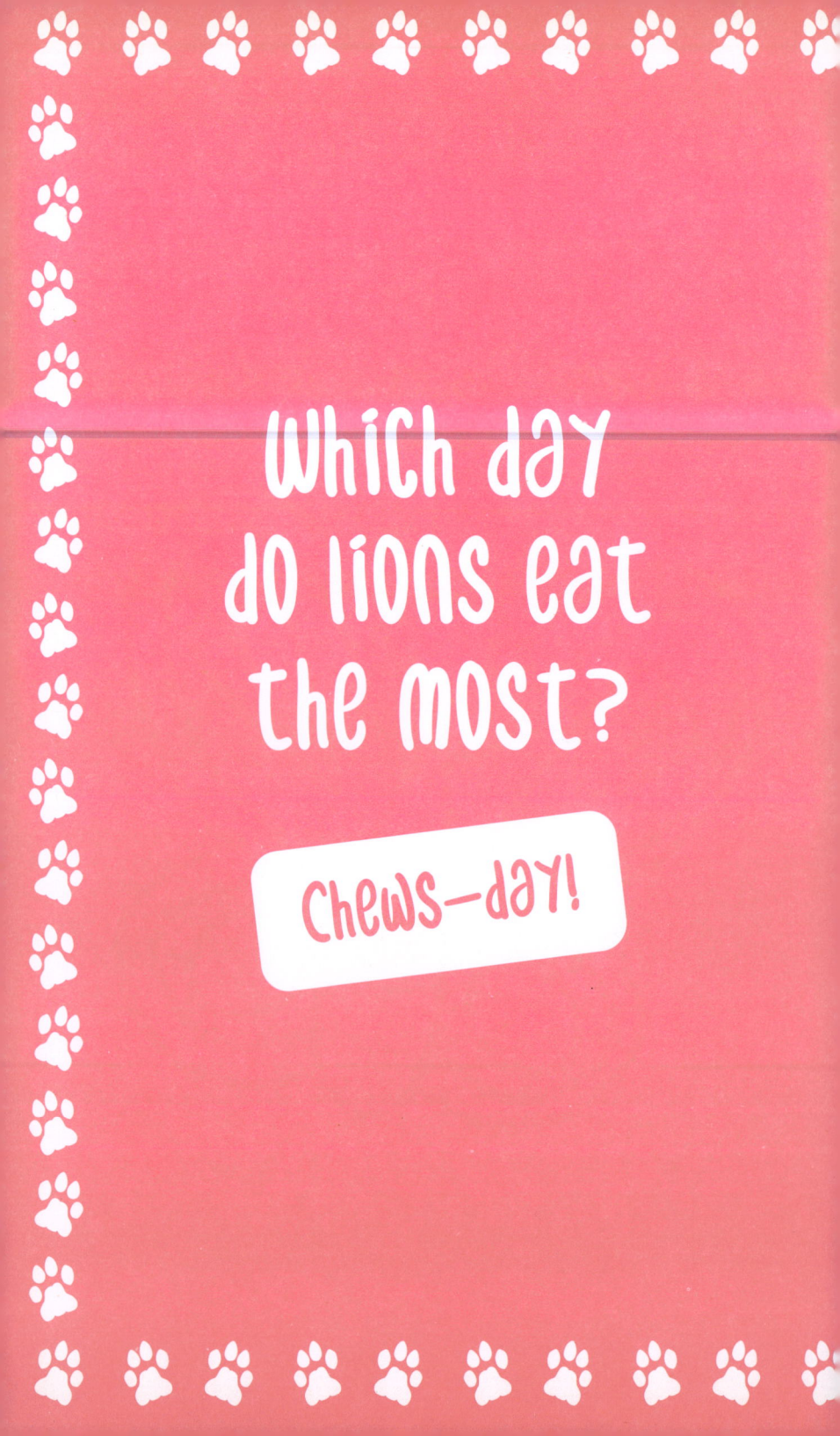

Chews–day!

What's my name?

....

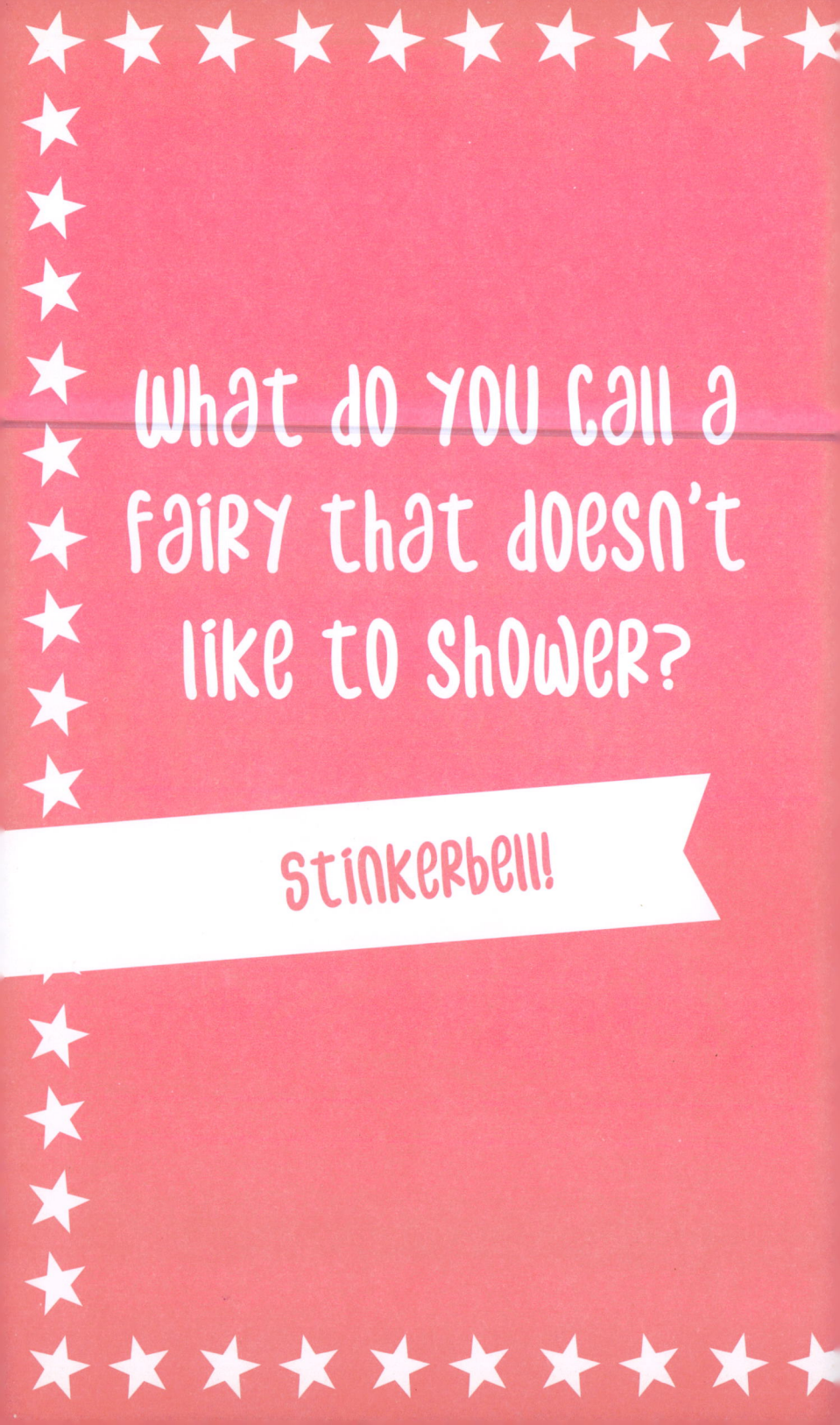

What do you call a fairy that doesn't like to shower?

Stinkerbell!

What's my name?

....

Where did the kittens go on a field trip?

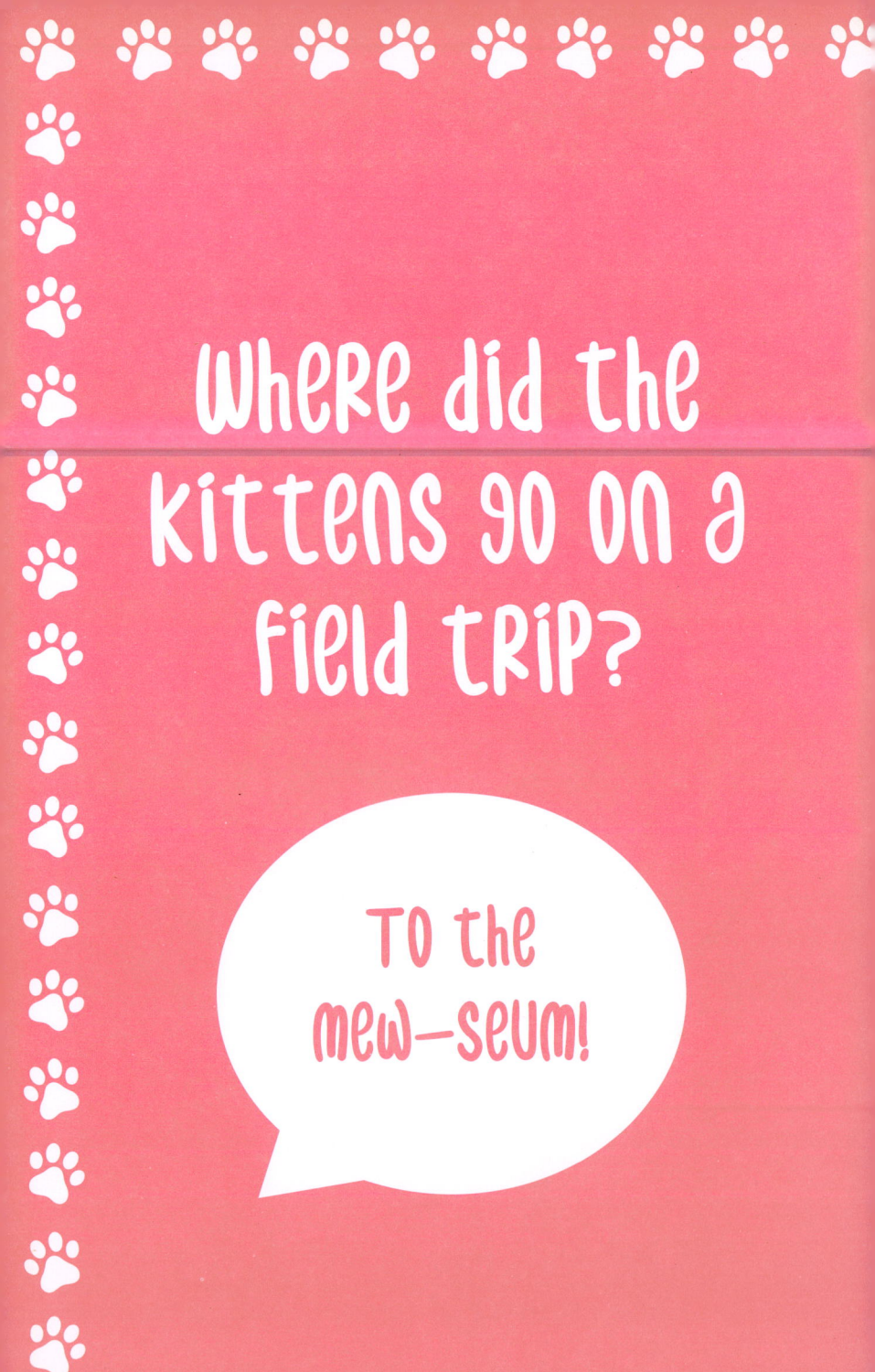

> To the mew-seum!

What's my name?

....

How do you make an octopus laugh?

You give it ten-tickles!

What's my name?

....

What kind of fish do penguins catch at night?

Starfish!

What's my name?

....

Why can't dragons play ice hockey?

The ice melts.

What's my name?

....

What do you call a hippo that won't clean its bedroom?

A hippopota-mess!

What's my name?

....

Why did the koala attend college?

> He had good koala-fications!

What's my name?

....

What do you call a guinea pig with three eyes?

A guinea piiig!

What's my name?

....

What do unicorns call their dads?

Pop-corn!

What's my name?

....

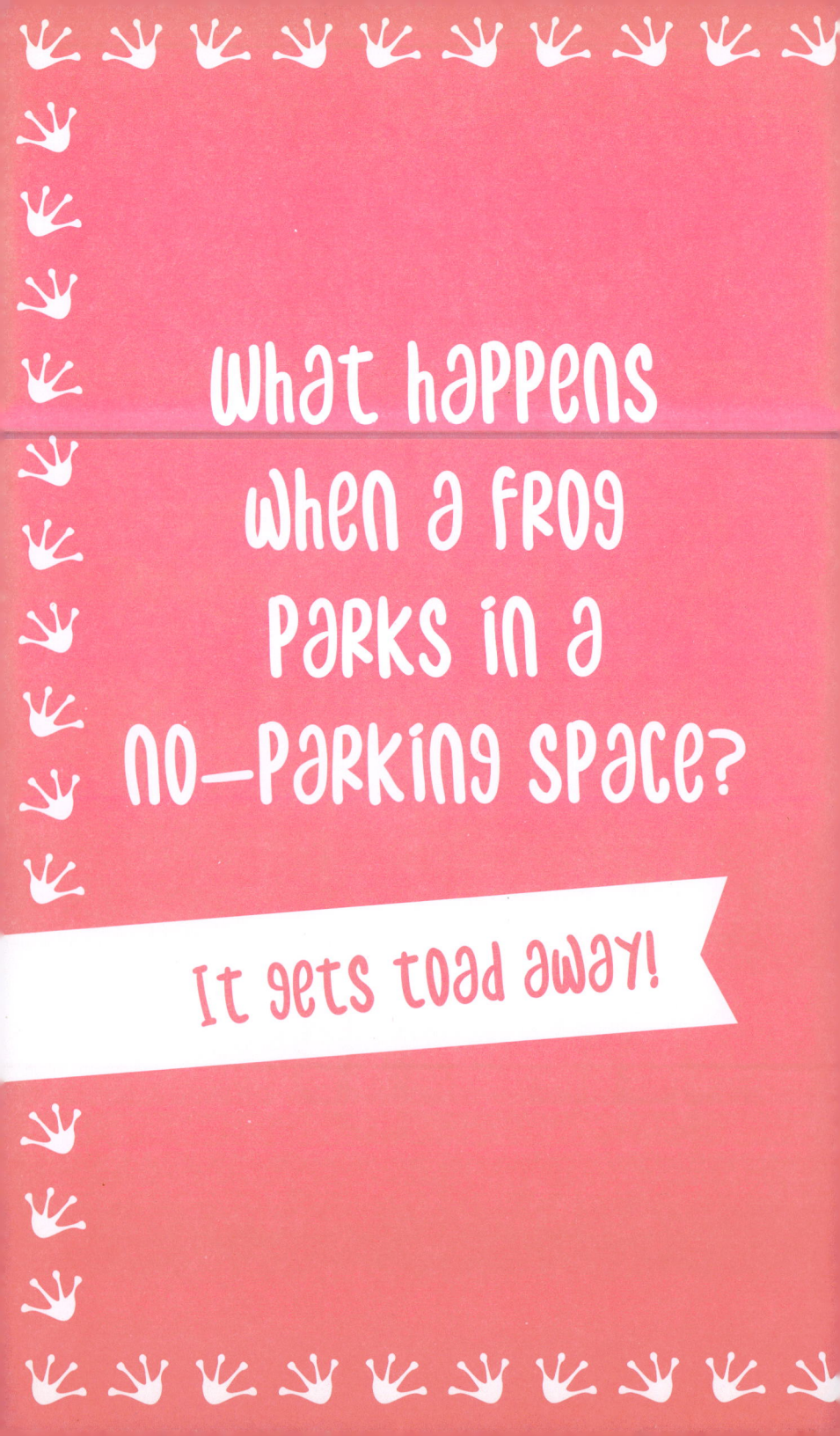

What happens when a frog parks in a no-parking space?

It gets toad away!

What's my name?

....

Write Your Own Cuter-Than-Cute Jokes Below!

Use these sketch pages to create your own cuter-than-cute drawings and works of art!

My super cute sketches...

My Super Cute Sketches...

My super cute sketches...

My Super Cute Sketches...

My super cute sketches...

My super cute sketches...

My Super Cute Sketches...

My super cute sketches...

My super cute sketches...

MY SUPER CUTE SKETCHES...

My super cute sketches...

My Super Cute Sketches...

My super cute sketches...

My super cute sketches...

My super cute sketches...

My super cute sketches...

My super cute sketches...

My super cute sketches...

My Super Cute Sketches...

My Super Cute Sketches...